SCHOLASTIC

READ & RESPOND

Bringing the best books to life in the classroom

Activities based on
THE WOLF WILDER
By Katherine Rundell

'A triumph'
Philip Pullman

THE
WOLF
WILDER

Katherine Rundell

Costa Children's Book Award Winner

BLOOMSBURY

FOR AGES 7–11

Published in the UK by Scholastic Education, 2020
Book End, Range Road, Witney, Oxfordshire, OX29 0YD
A division of Scholastic Limited
London – New York – Toronto – Sydney - Auckland
Mexico City – New Delhi – Hong Kong

SCHOLASTIC and associated logos are trademarks and/or registered trademarks of Scholastic Inc.

Printed and bound by Ashford Colour Press
© 2020 Scholastic Ltd
1 2 3 4 5 6 7 8 9   0 1 2 3 4 5 6 7 8 9

British Library Cataloguing-in-Publication Data
A catalogue record for this book is available from the British Library.
ISBN 978-1407-18383-1

Extracts from *The National Curriculum in England, English Programme of Study* © Crown Copyright. Reproduced under the terms of the Open Government Licence (OGL). http://www.nationalarchives.gov.uk/doc/open-government-licence/version/3

Authors Jillian Powell
Editorial team Vicki Yates, Suzanne Adams, Julia Roberts
Series designer Andrea Lewis
Typesetter QBS Learning
Illustrator Elizaveta Tretyakova

Acknowledgements
The publishers gratefully acknowledge permission to reproduce the following material:
Bloomsbury for the use of the text extracts and cover from *The Wolf Wilder* **by Katherine Rundell** (Bloomsbury, 2015). Text © Katherine Rundell. Reproduced by permission of the author c/o Rogers, Coleridge & White Ltd., 20 Powis Mews, London W11 1JN

How to use Read & Respond in your classroom...

Read & Respond provides teaching ideas related to a specific well-loved children's book. Each Read & Respond book is divided into the following sections:

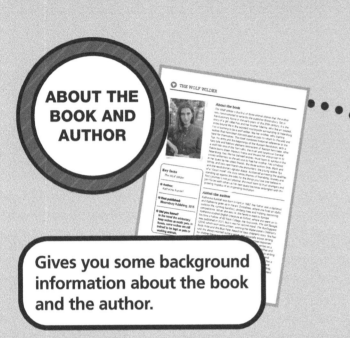

ABOUT THE BOOK AND AUTHOR

Gives you some background information about the book and the author.

GUIDED READING

Breaks the book down into sections and gives notes for using it with guided reading groups. A bookmark has been provided on page 12 containing comprehension questions. The children can be directed to refer to these as they read.

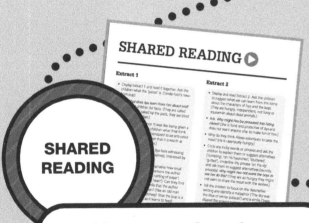

SHARED READING

Provides extracts from the children's book with associated notes for focused work. There is also one non-fiction extract that relates to the children's book.

GRAMMAR, PUNCTUATION & SPELLING

Provides word-level work related to the children's book so you can teach grammar, punctuation and spelling in context.

PLOT, CHARACTER & SETTING

Contains activity ideas focused on the plot, characters and the setting of the story.

GET WRITING

Provides writing activities related to the children's book. These activities may be based directly on the children's book or be broadly based on the themes and concepts of the story.

TALK ABOUT IT

Has speaking and listening activities related to the children's book. These activities may be based directly on the children's book or be broadly based on the themes and concepts of the story.

ASSESSMENT

Contains short activities that will help you assess whether the children have understood concepts and curriculum objectives. They are designed to be informal activities to feed into your planning.

> *The titles are great fun to use and cover exactly the range of books that children most want to read. It makes it easy to explore texts fully and ensure the children want to keep on reading more.*
>
> **Chris Flanagan, Year 5 Teacher, St Thomas of Canterbury Primary School**

Activities

The activities follow the same format:

- **Objective:** the objective for the lesson. It will be based upon a curriculum objective, but will often be more specific to the focus being covered.

- **What you need:** a list of resources you need to teach the lesson, including photocopiable pages.

- **What to do:** the activity notes.

- **Differentiation:** this is provided where specific and useful differentiation advice can be given to support and/or extend the learning in the activity. Differentiation by providing additional adult support has not been included as this will be at a teacher's discretion based upon specific children's needs and ability, as well as the availability of support.

The activities are numbered for reference within each section and should move through the text sequentially – so you can use the lesson while you are reading the book. Once you have read the book, most of the activities can be used in any order you wish.

Section	Activity	Curriculum objectives
Guided reading		Comprehension: To explain and discuss their understanding of what they have read.
Shared reading	1	Comprehension: To explain and discuss their understanding of what they have read.
	2	Comprehension: To discuss and evaluate how authors use language, including figurative language.
	3	Comprehension: To identify how language, structure and presentation contribute to meaning.
	4	Comprehension: To retrieve, record and present information from non-fiction; to explore the meaning of words in context.
Grammar, punctuation and spelling	1	Vocabulary, grammar and punctuation: To use expanded noun phrases to convey complicated information concisely.
	2	Vocabulary, grammar and punctuation: To understand and use adverbials, linking ideas across paragraphs.
	3	Vocabulary, grammar and punctuation: To use relative clauses beginning with who, which, where, when, whose, that or with an implied (i.e. omitted) relative pronoun.
	4	Vocabulary, grammar and punctuation: To indicate degrees of possibility using adverbs or modal verbs.
	5	Spelling: To distinguish between homophones and other words that are often confused.
	6	Spelling: To convert adjectives into verbs using suffixes.
Plot, character and setting	1	Comprehension: To identify and discuss conventions in and across a wide range of writing; to make comparisons across books.
	2	Comprehension: To summarise the main ideas drawn from more than one paragraph, identifying key details; Composition: To consider how authors have developed settings.
	3	Comprehension: To draw inferences, such as inferring characters' feelings, thoughts and motives from their actions, and to justify inferences with evidence.
	4	Comprehension: To explain and discuss their understanding of what they have read, maintaining a focus on the topic.
	5	Comprehension: To predict what might happen from details stated and implied.
	6	Comprehension: To draw inferences such as inferring characters' feelings, thoughts and motives from their actions, and to justify inferences with evidence.
	7	Comprehension: To provide reasoned justification for their views.
	8	Comprehension: To summarise the main ideas drawn from more than one paragraph, identifying key details that support the main ideas.

Section	Activity	Curriculum objectives
Talk about it	1	Spoken language: To articulate and justify answers, arguments and opinions.
	2	Comprehension: To infer characters' feelings, thoughts and motives from their actions, and to justify inferences with evidence; Spoken language: To participate in discussions.
	3	Spoken language: To use spoken language to develop understanding through speculating, hypothesising, imagining and exploring ideas.
	4	Spoken language: To participate in discussions.
	5	Spoken language: To articulate and justify answers, arguments and opinions.
	6	Spoken language: To give well-structured descriptions, explanations and narratives for different purposes, including for expressing feelings.
Get writing	1	Composition: To note and develop initial ideas, drawing on reading and research where necessary.
	2	Comprehension: To summarise the main ideas drawn from more than one paragraph.
	3	Comprehension: To discuss and evaluate how authors use language, including figurative language, considering the impact on the reader; Composition: To select appropriate vocabulary, understanding how such choices can enhance meaning.
	4	Composition: To select appropriate grammar and vocabulary; to use further organisational and presentational devices to structure text and to guide the reader.
	5	Composition: To select the appropriate form for the purpose of the writing.
	6	Comprehension: To predict what might happen from details stated and implied; Composition: To use other similar writing as models for their own.
Assessment	1	Comprehension: To identify and discuss themes; to make comparisons across books.
	2	Comprehension: To summarise the main ideas drawn from more than one paragraph.
	3	Composition: To précis longer passages; Comprehension: To summarise the main ideas drawn from more than one paragraph.
	4	Spelling: To understand the spelling of some words needs to be learned specifically. Comprehension: To check the book makes sense to them by exploring the meaning of words in context.
	5	Spoken language: To ask relevant questions to extend their understanding and knowledge.
	6	Comprehension: To explain and discuss their understanding of what they have read. Spoken language: To articulate and justify opinions.

Key facts
The Wolf Wilder

● **Author:**
Katherine Rundell

● **First published:**
Bloomsbury Publishing, 2015

● **Did you know?**
In the novel the aristocracy keep wolves as exotic pets. In Russia, some wolves are still trained to be kept as pets or working animals.

About the book

The Wolf Wilder is the first of three animal stories that the author was commissioned to write by the publisher Bloomsbury. Set in Revolutionary Russia in the early years of the 20th century, it is the story of a girl called Feo and her mother Marina, who live an isolated, snow-bound life in the wooded countryside surrounding St Petersburg. Feo is learning to be a wolf wilder, like her mother, who training wolves that have been domesticated as pets to return to the wild and fend for themselves. The novel combines historical references to the Tsar, his army and the beginnings of the Russian Revolution, with a fairy tale and folkloric element reminiscent of Russian fairy tales. After a wolf kills one of the Tsar's elks, the cruel and tyrannical General Rakov burns down Marina's home and throws her into prison in St Petersburg. Feo, like her beloved wolves, must learn to survive in the snowy wilderness as she sets out to free her mother. Feo is helped in her quest by her oldest friends, the three wolves Grey, Black and White, and two new friends she encounters, the young soldier Ilya and the revolutionary agitator Alexei. Acclaimed as having the qualities of a 'classic novel', the story carries themes of friendship, bravery and standing up against the odds for the things you love and believe in. Feo's journey is not just physical; she must learn to trust strangers and join forces with others as her own quest becomes entangled with the growing impetus of an impending revolution.

About the author

Katherine Rundell was born in Kent in 1987. Her father was a diplomat and Katherine grew up in Harare, Zimbabwe, where she lived an idyllic outdoor life, running barefoot, climbing trees and holding swimming competitions. When she was 14, the family moved to Europe. Katherine studied English Literature at Oxford, where she went on to become a Fellow of All Souls College. Her first book, *The Girl Savage*, was published in 2011, but it was her second novel, *The Rooftoppers* (2014) which won wide acclaim, winning the Waterstone's Children's Book Prize and the Blue Peter Award for best children's story. She has said she always wanted to be a writer, and especially enjoys writing for children because of their imaginative and interactive responses: 'You build them a house and they make it a castle'. She writes on a laptop in bed at home or in cafés or libraries, with lots of coffee and music, or the hubbub of café life in the background. As well as writing fiction and stage plays, she contributes to literary publications and radio programmes. Her pastimes include tightrope walking (she has a practice wire rigged up in her college rooms) and roof walking, and she says she begins every day with a cartwheel because, like reading, cartwheels can 'turn the world upside down and leave you breathless'.

GUIDED READING ▶

Cover and opening note

Begin by looking at the book cover and reading the blurb. Ask: *What can you deduce from them? What kind of story do you think this will be: an animal story, adventure, fantasy novel? Who is the story about?* (a girl called Feodora)

Begin reading the first section, 'A note on wolf wilders'. Ask the children to explain what a wolf wilder does. Have any of them heard of horse or dog whisperers? Ask: *How is this different and how similar?* (The whisperers tame or train animals; the wilder rehabilitates them for living in the wild.) Raise question 5 on the guided reading bookmark. Do they think this is a real or fantasy concept? Can they explain why? Note the humour and exaggeration in the detail. Raise question 1 on the bookmark.

Chapters 1, 2 and 3

Read the first chapter as far as 'someone knocking on the snow-blue door'. Ask: *What kind of story does the opening suggest?* (a fairy tale) *When and where is the story set?* (Russia, a century ago) Read on as far as 'You owe the Tsar a hundred roubles'. Ask the children if they can explain who the Tsar was (the ruler of Imperial Russia). *Why is he demanding money from Feo's mother?* (He believes that one of her wolves has killed the elk.) Continue reading to the chapter break. Refer to question 6 on the bookmark. Ask the children what Rakov demands (that from now on they shoot the wolves that people send for wilding). *What do they think happened to the 'rioters in St Petersburg'?* (They have been shot by the Tsar's army for rebelling.) Link to question 16 on the bookmark. Read to the end of the chapter and pause to ask the children for their first impressions of Feo and her mother, and of the life they live with the wolves. How would they describe Feo's character? (tough, fearless, stubborn, a bit wild?) Highlight the word '*lapushka*' and ask the children if they can suggest a translation (darling). Link to question 12 on the bookmark.

Continue reading through the next two chapters. Pause to ask why Marina tells Feo to pack a bag (in case she needs urgently to escape the General and his soldiers). Ask them to summarise skills the wilder must teach (to build a den, to run, to be fierce). Ask: *Why does Feo feel anxious when she thinks someone is watching them?* (She thinks it may be one of Rakov's spies.)

Chapters 4 and 5

Read on through Chapter 4. Ask: *Who was it who was watching Feo in the previous chapter?* (Ilya). Reflect how her senses are alert, like a wolf's, and she is completely at home in the environment. Ask: *What impresses Ilya about Feo?* (her strength, bravery, bond with the wolves?) Focus on the direct speech, considering questions 13 and 14 on the bookmark. *What convinces Ilya not to betray them to Rakov?* (He witnesses how tender the wolf is with her cub.) Carry on reading Chapter 5, pausing to note recurrent features in the narrative such as the use of similes to describe facial expressions (link to question 11 on the bookmark) and the use of chapter breaks to mark shifts in time. (Ask question 6 on the bookmark.) Read to the end of the chapter, highlighting the change in pace from the slower passages describing Feo's happy times with Ilya and the wolves, to the fast-paced episode when the soldiers arrive and attack. Refer to question 8 on the bookmark. Ask: *What has Feo done to Rakov?* (stabbed him in the eye) *What has happened to her mother?* (Marina has been arrested and taken away by the soldiers.). *What are the consequences for Feo?* (She is homeless and her mother is gone.)

Chapters 6, 7 and 8

Read Chapter 6 at pace. Ask: *What does Feo learn from Ilya?* (that the soldiers have burned down her home and her mother has been taken to jail in St Petersburg) Raise question 7 on the bookmark. Elicit that this is a turning point in the novel as Feo must now leave her home and set out on an adventure to rescue her mother. Bring out the contrast in the kind of skills and knowledge the two children have: Ilya knows about St Petersburg, the jail and the trials; Feo intimately knows the terrain and has practical skills like constructing a compass to lead them north. Use the dialogue between them to raise question 15 on the bookmark.

Begin reading Chapter 7, pausing to consider how Feo's knowledge of the terrain helps her: the fir trees are like an army of her own against the Tsar's men. As you reach the chapter end, again reflect on Ilya's familiarity with things that Feo has no knowledge of: the city, the ballet. Read Chapter 8 as far as 'This was something new.' Ask: *What is new?* (The wind has got up and the temperature has reached a new extreme – 'blind cold'.) *Can you explain what Marina taught Feo about fear?* (That it is not to be ashamed of, because it can guide you; it is *not* the same as cowardice.) Continue reading, checking that the children understand how the 'snow throne' offers relief by acting as a windbreak. Pause at the description of the village and ask the children if they can suggest what has happened: why are these 'ex-houses'? (They have been destroyed and burned by the Imperial Army.) Ask: *Why does Grey lie down with her nose pointing north?* (That is the direction for St Petersburg, where Marina is imprisoned.) Continue reading, pausing to ask the children to explain why Sasha is horrified when she sees Ilya's uniform. (She hates the Imperial Army because of what they have done to her village and her people.) *What do you imagine Feo means when she thinks to herself that Ilya is 'learning to be wild' and is 'in the pack'?* (He has left the army and is learning to survive with them out in the wilderness.) Consider how, although none of them has much, they are willing to share and exchange what they have. Ask: *What unites them?* (hatred of General Rakov) Read to the end of the chapter and ask: *What do we learn about Alexei?* (that he is an agitator – he wants to start a revolution, to overturn the rule of the Tsar and his army) Pause at the chapter's end to ask why Feo goes outside to sleep. (She is not used to being with other people; she feels more at home with the wolves in the snow.)

Chapters 9, 10 and 11

Read Chapter 9 at pace. Ask question 3 on the bookmark. Ask: *What does Alexei want Feo to do?* (to help inspire the people to rise up in a revolution, because she was brave enough to stand up to Rakov) *What will he do in exchange?* (tell her how to get through the city gates and give her food for the journey) Continue reading through Chapter 10. Ask: *What conflicting views of Feo do the villagers display?* (Some, like Grigory, view her as a dangerous witch-child; others as a heroine who attacked the evil Rakov.) Elicit that the requisitioners are working for the Tsar's army, stealing food and supplies from the villagers. *Which two things does Feo use to drive them away?* (snow and the wolves) Read Chapter 11 as far as the second chapter break. Ask: *Why is Feo feeling so uncomfortable and impatient?* (She is not used to socialising; she is anxious to waste no time in rescuing her mother.) *Do you think she is doing the right thing by going on her own?* Continue reading to the end of the chapter and ask why Feo feels so guilty and sad. (Grey has been shot and killed by Rakov.)

Chapters 12 and 13

Continue reading through Chapter 12 as far as the second chapter break. Ask the children why they think Feo suddenly bursts out crying (in her grief for Grey and also realising that she is not alone in her quest). Finish the chapter. Ask: *What are the children planning to do?* (get into the city, start a revolution and free Feo's mother) Contrast their bravery and enthusiasm with the caution of the adults. Link to question 17 on the bookmark. Highlight Ilya's remark at the end of the chapter. Ask: *Why does he think Feo has gone mad?* (He thinks there is no way they can appear like aristocrats.) Read on through Chapter 13 as far as the second chapter break. Pause to consider the 'fairy-tale' image of Feo, dressed in her makeshift finery, with the wolves, and remind the children of the fairy-tale thread that runs through the story. Link to question 10 on the bookmark. Finish reading the chapter and ask: *What do the children learn?* (that Marina is in the North Wing, her trial will be held when Rakov visits and she will face the death penalty) *How might Feo's impulsive nature let her down again and how does Alexei help her?* (She wants to try to rescue Marina right away; he persuades her they need the children to help them.) Reflect how once again Feo wants to 'go it alone' but that she must learn to accept the advice and help of others. Ask question 2 on the bookmark.

Chapter 14 to the end

Read Chapter 14 at pace. Ask: *How do the children plan to outwit the Imperial guards?* (by biting, kicking, using stinging nettles as a weapon and so on). Link to question 4 on the bookmark. *What do we learn about Ilya?* (that he is a promising dancer; that he is loyal to Feo and is prepared to sacrifice his own success to help her) Continue reading to the end of the novel. Check that the children understand what has happened to Rakov. (Feo has left him to the mercy of the wolves.) Ask question 9 on the bookmark. Point out the 'circular' structure with the fairy-tale language echoing the opening of the novel. *How is it a typical fairy-tale ending?* (They live happily ever after: Ilya has become a ballet dancer; Marina and Feo can live happily with the wolves, no longer threatened by Rakov). Invite feedback and first impressions of the novel.

The Wolf Wilder
By Katherine Rundell

Focus on...
Meaning

1. The novel combines real and fantastical elements. Identify examples of each.

2. Feo goes on a journey in more ways than one: can you explain the different journeys she takes?

3. When Alexei says 'Stories can start revolutions', what does he mean?

4. In what ways are Ilya and the other children 'wilded'?

Focus on...
Organisation

5. Consider the function of the note on wilders at the start of the story.

6. What function do the chapter breaks serve?

7. Identify key turning points in the narrative.

8. Identify passages where the pace of the narrative changes.

9. What is the style and function of the opening and closing paragraphs of the story?

The Wolf Wilder
By Katherine Rundell

Focus on...
Language and features

10. How does the narrative echo folkloric or fairy tales?

11. Explain how the author uses similes and metaphors.

12. Look out for Russian words in the narrative: what effect do they have?

13. How is direct speech used to convey character in the novel?

14. What effects does the author achieve by using incomplete sentences?

Focus on...
Purpose, viewpoints and effects

15. Consider where and how the author creates humour in the story.

16. Identify references to people or events that are based on historical fact.

17. How are children in the novel portrayed in contrast to adults?

SHARED READING ▶

Extract 1

- Display Extract 1 and read it together. Ask the children what the 'parcel' is. (Tenderfoot's new-born pup)

- Ask: *What does Ilya learn from Feo about wolf babies?* Let children list facts. (They are called pups, they are raised by the pack, they are blind for the first ten days.)

- Underline the sentence 'It was like being given a kingdom' and ask the children what they think it means. (Feo feels so honoured to be entrusted with the pup by its mother that it is worth as much to her as a kingdom.)

- How do the children think Ilya feels witnessing the birth? (amazed, overwhelmed, impressed by Feo's knowledge)

- Which words or phrases emphasise how small the pup is? Underline comparisons the author makes ('no louder than the rustling of paper'; 'its fingernail-sized beating heart'). Can they find another comparison or simile that the author uses to enhance description? ('like an old man dancing') What does it convey? (that the pup is a bit clumsy and chaotic as it learns to feed)

- How does the author emphasise similarities or the bond between the children and the wolves? (Tenderfoot entrusts her pup to Feo; Ilya's expression reminds Feo of Black's when he is hungry.)

- Ask: *What makes Ilya blush?* (Feo stares because he has shared something personal with her.)

- How do the children think the birth of the wolf pup affects Feo's friendship with Ilya? (They share something wild and magical, which brings them closer.)

Extract 2

- Display and read Extract 2. Ask the children to suggest what we can learn from this scene about the characters of Feo and the boys. (They are hungry, independent, not fussy or squeamish about dead animals.)

- Ask: *Why might Feo be provoked into biting Alexei?* (She is fond and protective of Ilya and does not want anyone else to make fun of him.)

- Why do they think Alexei volunteers to taste the meat? (He is ravenously hungry.)

- Circle any tricky words or phrases and ask the children to explain them or suggest alternatives ('fumbling', 'on his haunches', 'stuttered', 'gutted'). Underline the phrase 'on the sly', and ask them to suggest alternatives (secretly, privately). *Why might Feo not want the boys to see her do this?* (They are so hungry they might not want to share the meat with the wolves.)

- Tell the children to focus on the descriptive writing and identify a metaphor ('The sky was the blue of winter palaces') and a simile ('trees dipped like praying polar bears'). Ask: *How are they appropriate?* (They are features of cold, snowy landscapes.) Underline them and encourage children to consider how they help us visualise the scene.

- Underline the words 'Fictional food's not reliable' and ask them if they can explain what Alexei means. (You can't rely on recipes or food described in novels.)

- What do they understand by the words 'it only tasted blank'? (They had cooked it for so long, it had no taste to it.)

Extract 3

- Display and read Extract 3. Ask the children to summarise the action (the wolves attack Rakov and his soldier; Feo escapes by climbing a tree).

- Ask: *How does the author create a fast-moving pace?* Examine the length and structure of sentences, pointing out the repeated use of strong, active verbs ('shrieked', 'screamed', 'tore' and so on) and short, snappy sentences (for example, 'A shot rang out.')

- Challenge children to identify all the verbs that describe movement and underline them. ('rose', 'ran', 'reared', 'drumming', 'kicked out', 'leapt', 'turned', 'ran stumbling', 'ploughed', 'reached' 'scrambled', 'hauled', 'rocketed', 'kicked', 'gallop', 'tearing'). Reflect on the variety of words used and how they keep the description strong and vivid.

- Challenge the children to identify the different sounds that contribute to the drama. (The soldier's screams, the wolves' growling, the gun shot, the horse's shrieks and whinnies.)

- Ask: *Which phrases or sentences tell us how Feo is feeling?* (She tries to block out the terrible sounds; she screams but no sound comes out; her heart is beating very fast.)

- Ask: *Why is she so horrified when she hears the gunshot?* (She fears that Rakov has shot one of the wolves.)

- Challenge the children to identify figurative language, such as similes ('like a drunkard'; 'like being protected by a myth, by legend and spit'). Can they explain what these suggest? (The soldier sounds as if he is drunk when he screams out; the furious wolves that protect Feo seem like creatures of myth and legend.)

Extract 4

- Read Extract 4 together. Circle tricky vocabulary and ask the children to explain the meaning and suggest replacements. Encourage them to guess the meaning from the context or familiar usage. (For example, the context may help them guess 'hierarchy', 'gait', 'submissive'; thinking of the apex of a triangle may help them guess that an 'apex predator' is a predator at the top of the food chain.)

- Challenge the children to find adjectives used to describe wolves ('voracious', 'powerful', 'boisterous', 'dominant', 'submissive', 'endangered'). Repeat the exercise looking for nouns ('play-fighting', 'hunting unit', 'pack', 'hierarchy', 'gait', 'hackles' and so on). Reflect on technical terminology appropriate for factual description, such as 'gait' and 'citrine'. Ask: *Which phrase is a metaphor?* ('weapons in their armoury').

- Ask the children what they understand by re-wilding of wolves (the re-introduction of wolves to the wild). Ask: *How is this similar to or different from what Feo and Marina do in the novel?* (They train wolves domesticated as pets to go back to the wild.)

- Ask: *Which other facts about wolves are conveyed in the novel?* (The pups are blind, their eyes are blue at birth and turn yellow later, their senses are acute and so on.)

- Remind the children that Marina and Feo get into trouble with the Tsar because a wolf kills an elk. Ask: *Why do some people favour the re-wilding of wolves today?* (To keep down elk populations and protect the habitat of other animals.) *Why might the Tsar object to an elk being killed?* (He might hunt and kill them for sport.)

Extract 1

The parcel moved. It gave a cough, no louder than the rustling of paper. Feo could feel, through her skirt, its fingernail-sized beating heart.

'Oh!' said Feo. She bent her head to whisper. 'Welcome to the world, little one.' It was like being given a kingdom.

'Did you see that?' said Ilya. 'She gave him to you!'

'It's what they do in a pack. They raise the pups together.'

The look on the boy's face was so exactly like Black's when food was nearby that Feo was startled: it was hungry, and full of longing. She shifted in the snow to make room for him. 'Here. Come and see.'

'It's blind!' he gasped. 'Feodora, help it!'

'It's not blind. I mean – it's supposed to be. They don't open their eyes for about ten days.'

The pup's hips stuck up in two sharp points, as did his shoulders. He was black with white toes, and with smudges of grey on his chest. His eyes were closed, and as soon as Feo placed him at Tenderfoot's nipple his paws began to scrabble at her stomach, blindly coaxing out the milk. Feo laughed. It looked, irresistibly, like an old man dancing.

Ilya put out a hand to touch the pup, then hesitated, retracted it, sat on it. 'Look at that,' he breathed. 'The cub's drinking, isn't it?'

'Pup,' said Feo. 'Wolf babies are pups.'

'No more flesh on him than a kitchen table,' said Ilya. She stared, and he blushed. 'That's what my mother said about me when I was born. Before she died, not afterwards. My father said it'd be useful to have a thin child. Less to feed.' He moved closer.

Extract 2

Ilya struggled with the fire, fumbling with the matches in his cold hands. She watched Alexei, ready to bite him if he laughed – if anyone was laughing at Ilya, it would be her – but he only squatted on his haunches and stared at the world around them. She followed his gaze. The sky was the blue of winter palaces. The snow stretched, untouched, for miles, and the half-grown trees dipped like praying polar bears.

'That's a special kind of lovely,' said Ilya, looking up as the fire stuttered into life. 'Even if we get caught, I'm glad I came.'

Feo halved and gutted the jackdaw. They decided not to waste time plucking it; instead they sliced the skin off, and threw it to the wolves.

'How long do you need to cook jackdaw for?' she asked. 'A minute?'

'An hour?' said Ilya.

'Five hours?' said Alexei.

'We'll just have to taste it until it's ready,' said Ilya.

'I volunteer to do the tasting,' said Alexei.

None of them had ever cooked a jackdaw, but Ilya had read a story in which it had been done on sticks. 'Fictional food's not reliable,' Alexei objected, but Feo agreed with Ilya. They cut one half of the bird into slices and held these on sticks in the flickering tips of the flames, and the other half, still in a lump, they placed in the burning heart of the fire.

Feo threw a few scraps to the wolves on the sly.

The meat from the hot centre of the flames kept catching fire and having to be blown out.

'I think it's ready,' said Ilya. 'It looks cooked. It just doesn't look much like meat any more.'

Feo licked a chunk. It was vile on the outside, tasting of charcoal and stray feathers, but inside it only tasted blank.

Extract 3

The young soldier aimed his gun at her head but the wolf was on him. She rose on her hind legs and tore at his arm. He shrieked and ran, and Rakov's horse reared, its hooves drumming at the air.

Feo screamed and kicked out at the soldier holding her. As she did, Grey leapt at his shoulder and tore at his skin. The man screeched like a drunkard and turned, bleeding, clawing at the wolf with his nails. His face was lit up with rage and pain.

It was like being protected by a myth, by legend and spit.

Feo's legs loosened. She ran stumbling through the dark, heading for the pine trees with low branches, the pup in her arms, looking over her shoulder as she ploughed through the snow. She reached the nearest tree and scrambled against the trunk for a foothold, trying to close her ears to the hideous screaming and growling coming from below. Feo hauled herself into the lowest branches, and turned to see the second soldier run, stumbling, into the woods.

There were pine needles in her face. Her heart was beating so hard it shook her cloak.

A shot rang out.

'No!' Feo screamed, but it came out as a wordless roar.

There was a growl of pure animal fury and Black rocketed out of the shadows, followed by White, making straight for Rakov's feet. His horse let out a shriek, and Feo twisted in the tree to see him jerk sideways, away from the wolf, his gun dropping into the snow. The horse kicked and turned to gallop through the trees, tearing through the branches and whinnying in terror, the rider pressed flat against its back.

Extract 4

Re-wilding wolves

They are the voracious villains of our fairy tales and powerful predators in the wild. Like owls and hares, familiar creatures of folklore, wolves are active in the twilight and night hours. In the wild, they live in small packs, with adults and offspring forming strong nuclear families.

Deaf and blind at birth, pups feed by using their sense of touch and smell. As they grow, they use boisterous play-fighting to assess other family members. Establishing the hierarchy within a pack is an important part of becoming an effective hunting unit. Known as a 'route' when moving as a pack, wolves learn to communicate with each other to orchestrate a kill or protect their own. To survive and establish its place in the hierarchy, a young wolf must learn to read a combination of visual signals or cues from the face, posture, hair and tail. A dominant wolf which is preparing to attack, will bare its teeth and walk with a slow and purposeful gait, with its hackles raised and legs stiff. A submissive wolf will hide its teeth and keep its body low and its fur sleek, lowering its ears and tail. The tail is the most important cue of all: a raised tail will make the wolf look larger; a wagging tail communicates friendliness; while a stiff tail moving slowly can signal an attack.

Wolves possess intelligence and physical prowess. They can jump over two metres, and bite twice as powerfully as a police dog. Their senses are formidable weapons in their armoury, with noses that are a hundred times more sensitive than ours, and ears that can hear sounds from 16 kilometres away. Their eyes, blue at birth and turning citrine when they reach adulthood, possess acute day and night vision.

Although some species are endangered, wolves are coming back to parts of Europe, but their re-wilding is controversial. Some fear them. Others argue that these apex predators can balance the ecosystem, controlling elk populations that can otherwise destroy the habitats of animals including beavers, small mammals and songbirds.

GRAMMAR, PUNCTUATION AND SPELLING ▶

1. Describing nouns

Objective
To use expanded noun phrases to convey complicated information concisely.

What you need
Copies of *The Wolf Wilder*, Extract 4, photocopiable page 22 'Describing nouns'.

What to do

• Display an enlarged copy of Extract 4. Re-read the extract together, then circle the words 'hours', 'gait' and 'vision'. Ask the children if they can identify which part of speech they are (nouns). Examine the phrases which expand the nouns to describe them further: 'the twilight and night hours', 'a slow and purposeful gait', 'acute day and night vision'.

• Tell the children we call this kind of phrase an 'expanded noun phrase'. It is a neat, concise way of telling us more about the subject (noun).

• Challenge the children to find other expanded noun phrases in the extract, underlining or circling them ('the voracious villains'; 'powerful predators', 'strong nuclear families' and so on.)

• Note how the phrase gives us more information about the subject or noun in each case. Can the children suggest noun phrases to describe other nouns used in the extract? (For example, 'the tiny, newborn wolf pups'; 'its sharp, carnivorous teeth'; 'their keen, citrine eyes'.)

• Arrange the children into pairs and hand out photocopiable page 22 'Describing nouns'. Allow them time to fill in the sheet then bring the class back together to review it.

Differentiation
Support: Provide a list of possible nouns and adjectives to help children compose their phrases.

Extension: Challenge the children to write more noun phrases describing different nouns taken from the novel.

2. When, where, how?

Objective
To understand and use adverbials, linking paragraphs.

What you need
Copies of *The Wolf Wilder*, photocopiable page 23 'When, where, how?'

What to do

• Ask: *Which words open the novel?* ('Once upon a time'). Point out how the phrase acts as an adverb within the sentence, describing the verb that follows ('there was'). Explain that this kind of phrase is called an 'adverbial' and that it can describe when, where or how.

• Write examples of each on the board, underlining the adverbial phrase: '<u>Later that day</u>, Feo and her mother sat by the fire.' (when); '<u>In the chapel</u> lived a pack of three wolves.' (where); 'Alexei paced, <u>lion-like</u>, amongst the children.' (how).

• Find the context of the first two examples (Chapter 1). Discuss how these adverbials help link paragraphs: 'Later that day,' links the start of a new paragraph to an earlier action; and 'In the chapel lived a pack' links the new narrative about the wolves with the earlier description of the chapel.

• Provide pairs with photocopiable page 23 'When, where, how?' to complete together.

• Then challenge them to choose one of the sentences from the sheet to start a paragraph and write a short paragraph which could precede it – showing how the adverbial links the paragraphs.

Differentiation
Extension: Let pairs choose more sentences from the sheet and draft paragraphs that could precede them.

3. Useful relatives

Objective
To use relative clauses to join sentences.

What you need
Copies of *The Wolf Wilder*, flash cards with names of characters or subjects from novel.

What to do

- Arrange the class into pairs. Hand each pair a flash card with a name or topic from the novel (Feo, Marina, Ilya, Alexei, the castle, the wolves, and so on).

- Tell pairs to draft two short sentences about their subject. They can refer to the novel to help them. Model one pair on the board: 'Ilya was a soldier.'; 'Ilya wanted to be a ballet dancer.'

- When they have written their sentences, list on the board the relative pronouns 'who', 'which', 'where', 'when', 'whose', 'that'. Explain that they are now going to try joining their two sentences using a relative pronoun. Demonstrate on the board by writing 'Ilya was a soldier who wanted to be a ballet dancer.'

- Allow them time to write a sentence using a relative pronoun. Ask pairs to swap their flash cards to work on another subject.

- When they have finished, invite pairs to read aloud their sentences. Which relative pronouns from the list have been used? Are there any that have not been used? If so, encourage pairs to choose one of the names or subjects and compose a sentence aloud, using that pronoun.

- Reflect how relative pronouns are a useful way to join short sentences as they avoid repetition of the subject.

Differentiation
Support: As a class, draft pairs of short sentences then ask pairs to try joining them.

Extension: Challenge pairs to use all the listed pronouns.

4. Probably?

Objective
To indicate degrees of possibility using adverbs or modal verbs.

What you need
Copies of *The Wolf Wilder*.

What to do

- Invite two volunteers to read out the dialogue between Feo and Ilya in Chapter 4 (omitting the narrative and reading direct speech only) from '*Both* hands up!' as far as 'If you stayed still.'

- Highlight the adverbs 'Probably, actually.' Feo frequently adds 'probably' to her statements. Ask: *Why might she do this?* (perhaps when she is trying to appear brave and fearless but is really bluffing) List on the board the adverbs 'perhaps', 'maybe', 'probably', 'possibly' and 'certainly' and explain that we use them to indicate how likely something is.

- Focus on the verb tenses: point out how Feo uses the future tense 'will' and 'I'll', but Ilya says 'Could you…?', casting doubt on whether she really will kill him. List on the board the modal verbs 'will', 'would', 'may', 'might', 'shall', 'should', 'can' and 'could'. Tell the children that we also use verbs to indicate how possible or probable something is.

- Ask pairs to try reading aloud the same passage of dialogue, experimenting with adverbs and modal verbs to see which make it sound most likely and which least likely. For example, if Feo says 'I might kill you. Perhaps,' it sounds much less likely than if she says 'I will kill you. Certainly.'

Differentiation
Support: Let pairs experiment with changing the modal verbs in the dialogue then discuss as a shared class activity.

Extension: Challenge children to write the dialogue using different modal verbs and adverbs and to rank them to show degrees of possibility.

5. Sounding alike

Objective
To distinguish between homophones and other words that are often confused.

What you need
Copies of *The Wolf Wilder*, Extract 4.

What to do

- Display Extract 4. Circle the word 'gait' and ask a volunteer to suggest its homophone (gate). Challenge the children to use each word in a short sentence about something or someone from the novel, to bring out its meaning (for example, 'Grey moved with a slow, unsteady gait'; 'Feo saw the gate to the castle').

- Explain that they are going to try to identify homophones for other words in the extract, writing down the word and its homophone to show the difference in spelling.

- Ask pairs to work through the whole extract, finding as many words as they can which have homophones and writing them down (for example 'tales', 'hares', 'hours', 'route', 'read', 'cue', 'bare', 'gait').

- When they have compiled a list of words and their homophones, they should compose a pair of short sentences relating to the novel, using the word and its homophone to show the difference in spelling and meaning.

- Bring the class back together and invite volunteers from pairs to read their sentences, spelling the two homophones ('tails'/'tales', 'hares'/'hairs', 'hours'/'ours', 'route'/'root', and so on). Encourage the class to give feedback on which sentences work best and which were the trickiest homophones to find.

Differentiation
Support: Limit the task to finding the words and their homophones and then writing down the different meanings of each pair of words.

Extension: Encourage pairs to skim and scan a chapter of the novel to repeat the exercise.

6. Changing parts

Objective
To convert adjectives into verbs using suffixes.

What you need
Copies of *The Wolf Wilder*, photocopiable page 24 'Changing parts'.

What to do

- Focus on the idea of 'wilding' in the novel; reflect that the author invents the term 'wolf wilder' to describe someone who helps tame wolves to re-enter the wild.

- Point out that the word 'wild' can function as a noun, adjective, adverb and even a verb (although more frequently as 're-wilding' as in Extract 4).

- Arrange the children in pairs and challenge them to draft short sentences about wolves using 'wild' as all the different parts of speech. For example, 'Wolves live in the wild' (noun); 'Wolves are wild animals' (adjective); 'The wolves ran wild' (adverb); 'Feo wilds wolves' (verb).

- Bring the class together to share ideas.

- Reflect that some adjectives, like 'wild', keep the same form as a verb – for example: 'ready', 'complete' and so on. For another group of adjectives, we add letters at the end (a suffix) to turn them into the verb: for 'soft' we add '-en' (soften). For 'just' we add '-ify' (justify).

- Hand out photocopiable page 24 'Changing parts' for pairs to complete.

- Allow them time to complete the task then bring the class back together. Invite volunteers to identify the adjectives and read out their completed sentences.

Differentiation
Support: Let children use dictionaries.

Extension: Challenge pairs to find more adjectives and verbs that follow the same pattern to add to the sheet.

 # Describing nouns

- Match each phrase to a noun to compose an expanded noun phrase used in the novel. Draw a line between the phrase and the noun it describes.

phrase	noun
dark and stormy	animals
powdery	war cry
a choked	sneezes
tiny, doll-size	girl
freshly laundered	snow
two magnificent gold-anointed	shirt

- Choose two of the noun phrases and use each in a sentence which includes another expanded noun phrase of your own.

1. _____

_____

_____

2. _____

_____

_____

When, where, how?

- Write an adverbial to complete each sentence. You can use the list below to help you or think of your own.
- Write in the box what kind of adverbial it is.

when, where or how?

1.	_____, the storm gave a roar.
2.	The wolves formed a wreath _____
3.	_____ Alexei stopped talking.
4.	The children found shelter from the wind _____
5.	Feo snatched the pup up _____
6.	_____, Feo climbed onto Black's back.

behind them	suddenly, abruptly	by the scruff	around the grave	very slowly
		behind the snow throne	at that moment	

Changing parts

- Circle an adjective in the first sentence in each pair.
- Make the adjective into a verb by adding the correct suffix (you may need to change the ending of the root word first). Then use the verb to complete the second sentence.

Suffixes			
-ate	-en	-ify	- ise

1. Feo tries to make the bandage tight for White.

Feo tries to _____ the bandage for White.

2. Grey became weak and died.

Grey began to _____ and died.

3. Aristocrats keep wolves as domestic pets.

Aristocrats _____ wolves as pets.

4. Rakov's anger became more intense after Feo's attack.

Rakov's anger began to _____ .

5. Alexei has revolutionary beliefs.

Alexei wants to _____ society.

6. Sasha adds sugar to make the apples sweet.

Sasha added sugar to _____ the apples.

PLOT, CHARACTER AND SETTING ▶

1. A fantastic adventure

Objectives
To identify and discuss conventions in and across a wide range of writing; to make comparisons across books.

What you need
Copies of *The Wolf Wilder*, photocopiable page 29 'A fantastic adventure'.

What to do

- Ask the children which genre/s they think the novel fits into and why. Discuss the different aspects of the novel. It falls into the adventure genre because Feo has to set out on a dangerous and eventful journey to achieve her goal. It also has elements of folklore, fairy tale and fantasy in the wild, dramatic setting and in the concept of wilding pet wolves, but it is set in a real place and time – Imperial Russia under the Tsar, over a hundred years ago.

- Begin by brainstorming together some typical features of an adventure story, encouraging children to cite other novels or films as examples (a likeable lead character; a quest or journey; dangers or villains and obstacles to overcome, and so on). List ideas on the board.

- Ask pairs to complete photocopiable page 29 'A fantastic adventure', referring to the novel for information.

- Bring the class back together and discuss how far the novel is a classic adventure story and in what ways it deviates – for example, the lead character goes on a journey or quest, but she becomes swept up in the revolutionary fervour or unrest that led to the Russian Revolution.

Differentiation
Support: Consider the questions on the sheet as a shared activity, before pairs complete it.

Extension: Encourage pairs to note key ingredients of the fantasy/historical aspects of the novel.

2. A snowy setting

Objectives
To summarise the main ideas drawn from more than one paragraph, identifying key details; to consider how authors have developed settings.

What you need
Copies of *The Wolf Wilder*.

Cross-curricular links
Geography, history

What to do

- Tell the children they are going to focus on when and where the story is set. Discuss key facts together: Russia, in the countryside, about a hundred years ago under the Tsar. The challenge is to retrieve all the information they can from the novel about the time and place of the novel's setting. Before they begin, ask them to suggest topics to focus on (for example, the landscape or terrain, the weather or climate, the city of St Petersburg, the Tsar and his army, the Russian language). Write their suggestions on the board.

- Arrange the children into small groups and assign them one of the topics. Tell them to skim and scan the novel for any facts they can find for their topic, and to list what they find.

- Bring the class back together and, using the headings on the board, share ideas. Discuss what most helps to convey a sense of place in the novel (including the use of Russian words, names and terms, and descriptions of the landscape); and what conveys a sense of the time or period in history (including references to events, transport such as horses and sleds, clothes and so on).

Differentiation
Support: Provide groups with chapter and page references to locate relevant information.

Extension: Challenge groups to find out more facts about one of the topics using their own research.

3. Wolf girl

Objective

To draw inferences, such as inferring characters' feelings, thoughts and motives from their actions, and to justify inferences with evidence.

What you need

Copies of *The Wolf Wilder*.

What to do

- Tell the children that they are going to focus on the lead character in the novel, Feodora. Ask: *Which words could we use to describe her?* (dark, fierce, wild, brave, impulsive). If possible, encourage a range of words suggesting behaviour and personality as well as appearance.

- Write three headings on the board, 'Appearance', 'Dialogue' and 'Action', and suggest that all three are used by authors to convey character. Ask pairs to skim and scan the first chapter of the novel to write down examples under each heading. Bring the class back together and note ideas on the board (for example, Appearance: 'dark and stormy'; Dialogue: 'Get out!'; Action: she plays chase with a wolf).

- Encourage the children to think how together the different elements build our picture of Feo as a girl who is brave, feisty and a bit wild. Ask: *Are there any points in the chapter where we see a more vulnerable side to Feo?* (For example, when she is holding the ski as a weapon, she hopes Rakov cannot see her eyes prickling with tears.)

- Assign pairs three or four chapters of the novel and challenge them to note more examples under each heading which help convey character.

- Bring the class back together and share ideas.

Differentiation

Support: Let pairs work on just one of the three categories.

Extension: Let children perform the same task for another character, such as Ilya or Alexei.

4. Talkative weather

Objective

To explain and discuss their understanding of what they have read, maintaining a focus on the topic.

What you need

Copies of *The Wolf Wilder*, photocopiable page 30 'Talkative weather'.

What to do

- Tell the children they are going to focus on snow and how it features in the novel, in descriptions of the setting and also in the plot. Invite volunteers to cite memorable scenes when snow features. Ask: *How do you think Feo views snow: as a friend or a foe?* Encourage them to support their answers with reasons.

- Challenge pairs to list as many ways as they can that snow is part of Feo's life. (For example: she uses skis to get around; she cools her cheeks with snow when she blushes; she teaches the wolves to make snow dens; she roars into the snow when Grey dies and so on.)

- Bring the class back together to share ideas. Ask: *What do you think Feo means when she calls snow 'the most talkative weather there is'?* (That when you are as familiar with the snow as she is, you can learn a lot from it.) *Can you suggest any practical examples?* (When she first arrives at the ruined castle, it tells her no one has been there for a year.)

- Hand out photocopiable page 30 'Talkative weather' and ask pairs to complete it. Bring the class back together to share findings.

Differentiation

Support: Provide chapter references for key information (Chapters 3, 8 and 10).

Extension: Challenge pairs to draft a paragraph about snow in Feo's own words.

5. Clever clues

Objective
To predict what might happen from details stated and implied.

What you need
Copies of *The Wolf Wilder*, photocopiable page 31 'Clever clues'.

What to do

- Ask the children to recall what happens in the first chapter. What is the purpose of Rakov's visit? (To extract payment for the dead elk and warn Marina and Feo that they must shoot any wolves sent to them, or face punishment by the Tsar.) Ask: *What questions does this raise in the reader's mind? Do we think Marina and Feo will obey him – if not, why not?* Point out that the author immediately sets up a conflict which must be resolved within the novel: Marina and Feo will not give up the wolves, which will put them at risk from the Tsar and his army – what will happen to them?

- Suggest that authors raise questions like this to engage us as readers: they keep us guessing and wanting to find out answers. During the novel they may also seed clues, allowing us as readers to predict what might happen.

- Arrange the children into pairs and hand out photocopiable page 31 'Clever clues'. When complete, bring the class back together to review their findings. Discuss how sometimes the author implies rather than states what will happen (and we must predict or infer it) as when Feo leaves Rakov alone to the mercy of the wolves.

Differentiation
Support: Check that pairs understand the task by attempting one or two as a shared activity.

Extension: Challenge pairs to extend the photocopiable sheet by identifying more clues and predictions.

6. Agitators all!

Objective
To infer characters' feelings, thoughts and motives from their actions, and to justify inferences with evidence.

What you need
Copies of *The Wolf Wilder*.

Cross-curricular links
History, PSHE

What to do

- Ask the children if they can explain what an agitator is in the context of the novel. Then read aloud Ilya's explanation from Chapter 8: *'a person who acts against the Tsar'.*

- Using that definition, ask them to suggest characters in the novel who act as agitators (Marina, Feo, Ilya, Alexei, the children). Write suggestions on the board.

- Arrange the children into small groups and assign each group one of the named characters. They should discuss how that character acts against the Tsar, what risks they take, and why they take them (their motivation for being an agitator). Encourage the children to consider the level of risk that each character runs (arrest? death sentence?) and why they think they are willing to take those risks.

- Bring them back together to discuss their ideas, writing key notes for each character on the board.

- Ask: *Who do you think is the main 'ring leader' in their actions?* (Alexei) *How is his motivation different from Feo's?* (He wants to start a revolution; she wants to free her mother.) *Why does Alexei enlist Feo in his cause?* (He thinks she will inspire others with her bravery.) *How does helping him in turn help Feo?* (He brings the children along with him.)

Differentiation
Support: Write ideas about one character on the board before groups begin.

Extension: Ask children to research more about the agitators who started the Russian Revolution.

7. Tough children

Objective
To provide reasoned justification for their views.

What you need
Copies of *The Wolf Wilder*.

Cross-curricular link
PSHE

What to do

- Tell the children to focus on the role that children play in the novel. Discuss how children are key characters: the lead characters Feo, Ilya and Alexei are all children; it is a group of children who set out with Feo to free her mother and start a revolution.

- Write on the board a quote by Marina: 'Children are the toughest creatures on the planet. They endure.' (Chapter 8) Ask a volunteer to explain what they think Marina means and say whether they agree with her. Encourage them to support their answers with evidence from the novel or real life.

- Ask pairs to note all the ways that children demonstrate how strong or tough they are in the novel (for example, Feo attacks Rakov; Ilya defies the General's orders; the village children storm the city, and so on).

- Bring the class back together and share ideas. Discuss the qualities children demonstrate in their actions – toughness, determination, inventiveness and so on. Ask: *Why do you think children might be more fearless than the adults?* (Perhaps because they are less aware of the risks?)

Differentiation

Support: List together on the board key actions that children carry out in the novel, then encourage pairs to discuss the qualities they show.

Extension: Let pairs discuss the merits and flaws in the children's approach as opposed to the adults'.

8. Russian homes

Objective
To summarise the main ideas drawn from more than one paragraph, identifying key details that support the main ideas.

What you need
Copies of *The Wolf Wilder*.

Cross-curricular link
Geography

What to do

- Tell the children that they are going to focus on the different homes depicted in the novel, and what they tell us about the way the Russian people lived at that time in history. Challenge them to recall the homes described: the wooden house where Feo and her mother live (Chapter 1), Sasha and Alexei's house (Chapter 8) and the ruined castle where Feo and Marina finally come to live (Chapters 12 and 15).

- Discuss some different aspects of the home to consider, writing ideas on the board (for example: building materials used, outside, inside, furniture, food and so on).

- Arrange the children into small groups and assign them one of the three homes, ensuring all three of them are covered.

- Allow them time to skim and scan the relevant chapters, noting information under the suggested headings, then bring the class back together to share and compare ideas. Note the use of local materials for building (timber, sheep's wool and so on) and the colourful paint and furniture used to make the homes feel warm and cosy although the climate outside is so harsh. Finally, remind the children of the thickly carpeted houses of the aristocrats in St Petersburg (opening section, 'A note on wolf wilders') and contrast their opulence and grandeur with the houses lived in by the villagers.

Differentiation

Support: Provide page references to help children locate information.

Extension: Let children use their notes to draft a paragraph describing one of the houses.

A fantastic adventure

- Answer the questions using your knowledge of the novel.

Name of lead character

_____

What is the goal of their journey or quest?

_____

_____

_____

List three dangers or obstacles facing them along the way.

1. _____

_____

2. _____

_____

3. _____

_____

Who or what helps them in their quest?

_____

_____

_____

How do they reach their goal in the end?

_____

_____

_____

 # Talkative weather

- Write a short paragraph explaining how snow is important to the setting of the novel.

_____

_____

_____

_____

_____

- Explain three ways snow features in the plot. (clues: to make a compass/weapons/ a shelter)

1. _____

_____

_____

_____

2. _____

_____

_____

_____

3. _____

_____

_____

_____

Clever clues

- Draw a line to match two clues and write what we predict will happen.

Clues

Clues		What can we predict?
Feo is impatient to leave for St Petersburg to free Marina.	Ilya warns Feo that Rakov and his men are on their way.	
Ilya hints he never wanted to be a soldier.	Ilya is sleeping and Alexei is busy partying.	
Feo tells Rakov wolves don't read the Bible.	Feo leaves the wolves in the prison cell with Rakov.	
Marina tells Feo to pack a bag and leave it by the door.	Ilya shows he is a brilliant dancer.	

TALK ABOUT IT ▶

1. Wild pets

Objective
To articulate and justify answers, arguments and opinions.

What you need
Copies of *The Wolf Wilder*.

Cross-curricular links
Science, geography

What to do

- Re-read 'A note on wolf wilders'. Ask: *Do you think Russians really kept wolves in this way a century ago? Why might keeping wolves as domestic indoor pets be cruel?* (Because they are wild animals, and it would deprive them of their natural instinctive behaviour.)

- Suggest that although the author has developed a fictional concept, there *are* exotic animals, including wolves, which people can get licenses to keep as pets. Together, list examples: lions, tigers, crocodiles, snakes, lemurs and so on. Reflect that domesticated animals like dogs and cats have traits that are different from wild animals – they form a bond with their owners. Exotic species, especially those that are solitary rather than social (like crocodiles), have different needs. There is also an illegal trade in some species, with animals captured from the wild and sold as pets.

- Ask small groups to discuss the idea of keeping exotic animals. They should consider: *What are the pros and cons? What are the risks to the owners and to the animals?* (For example, pets may injure owners, or be abandoned or die when their owners can't meet their needs.)

- Bring the class together to share ideas.

Differentiation
Support: Provide topics to consider: a wild animal's needs; potential problems, etc.

Extension: Let groups prepare a short presentation discouraging people from owning exotic pets.

2. Feo's feelings

Objectives
To infer characters' feelings, thoughts and motives from their actions, and to justify inferences with evidence; to participate in discussions.

What you need
Copies of *The Wolf Wilder*.

Cross-curricular link
PSHE.

What to do

- Tell the children to focus on Feo's character. Remind them of the work they did in the lesson 'Wolf girl'. Recall adjectives they used to describe her ('strong', 'brave', 'fierce 'and so on). Ask: *Can you suggest episodes or encounters in the story when Feo demonstrates these qualities?* (when she is playing with the wolves; when she stands up to General Rakov; when she first meets the young soldier, Ilya) Write their suggestions on the board.

- Ask: *When does Feo appear less confident or brave, or seem uncomfortable?* (For example, when she is asked to dance, or when she has to address the children.) Again, note their ideas.

- Ask small groups to scan the novel to find situations where Feo feels afraid or unsure of herself, then discuss why they think she feels like that, when she is brave in so many other ways.

- Share ideas as a class. Elicit that Feo feels uncomfortable in social situations because she lives a solitary life in the woods with her mother, the wolves and the snow. Ask: *What happens to change her outlook?* (She makes friends with Ilya and learns to accept help from Alexei and the village children.)

Differentiation
Support: List episodes on the board for groups to discuss.

3. Whisperers and wilders

Objective
To use spoken language to develop understanding through speculating, hypothesising, imagining and exploring ideas.

What you need
Copies of *The Wolf Wilder*, photocopiable page 35 'Whisperers and wilders'.

Cross-curricular link
Science

What to do

- Ask if children are familiar with the terms 'horse' or 'dog whisperer'. Challenge a volunteer to explain what they do (they tame or train the animal through gentle communication). Ask: *How is this different from what Feo and her mother do as 'wilders'?* (They teach tame or domesticated wolves to be wild again, so that they can fend for themselves and live back in the wild).

- Hand out photocopiable page 35 'Whisperers and wilders' and ask pairs to discuss each question together before writing their answers.

- Bring the class back together to share ideas. Discuss together the idea of natural behaviours in animals (such as living alone or in social groups, hunting or foraging for food, making nests or dens, finding a mate and so on). Suggest that both whisperers and wilders must learn those behaviours so that they can communicate and train the animals.

- Focus on the idea of wilding. Ask children what they know about re-wilding, linking back to Extract 4 in Shared reading. Can they suggest when and how animals are re-wilded? (Some endangered species are bred in captivity then re-wilded; other animals may need to be re-wilded after they have been taken in for veterinary care or treatment.)

Differentiation
Support: Re-read Chapter 3 and as a class discuss the term 'whisperer' together before they begin work.

Extension: Let pairs discuss concepts of whispering and wilding, preparing a spoken definition for each.

4. Rules and revolutions

Objective
To participate in discussions.

What you need
Copies of *The Wolf Wilder*, photocopiable page 36 'Rules and revolutions'.

Cross-curricular link
History

What to do

- Remind the children that Alexei tries to persuade Feo to address the people by saying 'Stories can start revolutions.' Ask them what they think he means (that hearing about personal experiences can trigger the feelings that will bring political and social changes).

- Discuss and note on the board key facts about the Russian Revolution, encouraging volunteers to suggest information. Explain that the discontent among the workers that led to the revolution had been building since the early 1900s. In 1905, Russian soldiers had shot at crowds, killing people who were protesting on the streets of Petrograd (St Petersburg) against poor living and working conditions. The Tsar finally abdicated his throne in 1917, when the Bolsheviks, the party of the ordinary working people founded by Lenin, took control of the government.

- Discuss how the novel reflects real events in Russia, with the actions of the Tsar and his soldiers creating discontent and unrest among the people. Hand out photocopiable page 36 'Rules and revolutions' and ask the children to complete the task, working in pairs to skim and scan the novel and make notes under each heading.

- Bring the class back together and, using their notes, discuss what the novel tells us about the people and events of the period.

Differentiation
Support: List on the board the relevant sections of the book to help children complete each part of the sheet.

Extension: Encourage groups to research more about the revolution.

5. Feo and friend

Objective
To articulate and justify answers, arguments and opinions.

What you need
Copies of *The Wolf Wilder*, photocopiable page 37 'Feo and Ilya'.

Cross-curricular link
PSHE

What to do

- Begin by asking the children what they think makes a good friend. Discuss ideas together, writing suggestions on the board (someone who enjoys the same things as you do, someone who shares experiences/belongings with you, someone who makes you laugh, someone you trust, someone who helps you or sticks up for you and defends you). Discuss how we make new friends: for example, when we are brought together by going to the same school or activity, or doing the same hobbies or sports, then discover that we enjoy each other's company and share interests.

- Arrange the children into pairs and challenge them to think how Feo and Ilya become friends, and how they demonstrate their friendship in the novel (they share experiences like seeing the pup born and sheltering in the snow throne; they share food; they protect each other from Rakov, and so on).

- Bring the class back together and share key ideas.

- Hand out photocopiable page 37 'Feo and Ilya' and challenge children to complete the sheet individually. Invite volunteers to read their statements, linking their ideas back to evidence in the novel. Encourage feedback on which are most convincing and why.

Differentiation

Support: Let children work in pairs on the photocopiable sheet, each voicing one character.

Extension: Let pairs discuss different kinds of friendship shown in the novel, for example, Feo's friendship with the wolves.

6. Revolutionary feelings

Objective
To give well-structured descriptions, explanations and narratives for different purposes, including for expressing feelings.

What you need
Copies of *The Wolf Wilder*, children's completed photocopiable page 36 'Rules and revolutions'.

Cross-curricular link
History

What to do

- Tell the children they are going to focus on how characters feel under the rule of the Tsar and his army in the novel. Remind them of what they found out in the lesson 'Rules and revolutions' and hand out the children's completed sheets for them to refer to.

- Re-read together some of the sections of the novel where we see the effects of the soldiers' actions on the characters. For example, soldiers burning homes (Feo's home, Chapter 5), killing animals and arresting people (Grigory's account, Chapter 10), and requisitioners seizing families' food and possessions (Yana and the requisitioners, Chapter 10).

- Discuss together the feelings aroused in the working people because of their treatment by the authorities (fear, frustration, resentment, anger).

- Ask pairs to choose one of the incidents and imagine they are one of the affected characters (Feo, Marina, Grigory, Alexei, Yana and so on). Ask them to re-read the incident together and prepare a brief oral account of what happened from that character's point of view, focusing on how they felt at each stage. (For example, 'I was terrified when I heard the soldiers riding into the village.')

- Bring the class back together and ask children to share their character's narrative.

Differentiation

Support: Provide notes on a particular incident and help children infer characters' feelings at each stage.

Extension: Challenge pairs to explore more than one incident and develop their character accounts into a short performance.

Whisperers and wilders

- Discuss each question and write your answers.

What does an animal whisperer do?

_____

What does an animal wilder do?

_____

What kind of animal might need a whisperer?

_____

What kind of animal might need a wilder?

_____

List three things a whisperer might try to do:

1. _____

_____

2. _____

_____

3. _____

_____

List three things a wilder might try to do:

1. _____

_____

2. _____

_____

3. _____

_____

Rules and revolutions

- Write some facts we learn in the novel about the following

The Tsar *What kind of man was he? What did the people think of him?*

The Tsar's army *How did the army behave towards the Russian people?*

Kresty Jail *Who was sent there and why?*

The requisitioners *Who were they and what did they do?*

Crimes and punishments *What were people arrested for and how were they punished?*

Feo and Ilya

- Write three things Feo might say about Ilya.

The best thing
about Ilya is

I like Ilya because

Ilya is a good
friend to me because

- Write three things Ilya might say about Feo.

I like Feo because

The best thing
about Feo is

Feo is a good
friend to me because

GET WRITING ▶

1. A new saint

> **Objective**
> To note and develop initial ideas, drawing on reading and research where necessary.
>
> **What you need**
> Copies of *The Wolf Wilder*, photocopiable page 41 'A new saint'.
>
> **Cross-curricular link**
> RE

What to do

- Re-read Chapter 4 from 'Tenderfoot gave a breathy howl' to 'They raise the pups together'. Focus on Feo's prayer to 'whichever saint took care of wolf pups and vulnerable, snuffling things.' Ask the children to suggest what Feo's prayer might be (for the second pup to be born alive and to thrive). Remind them how she also prays to 'the saints of good aim and wild ideas' when she breaks the icicles to attack Rakov (Chapter 7).

- Ask if any of them can explain what a saint is. Explain that, while the word 'saint' comes from Christianity, many different faiths or religions believe that people who live an exceptionally good life and perform good deeds should be given a special status after they die (these could be Sikh 'gurus' or Islamic 'walis'). Refer to some famous saints Feo might be familiar with: St Francis of Assisi or St Peter. Discuss how people may pray and ask for protection from saints, as Feo does.

- Tell them they are going to develop Feo's idea of the saint. Hand out photocopiable page 41 'A new saint' and ask pairs to complete it.

- Bring the class together, inviting volunteers to describe their saint.

> **Differentiation**
> **Support:** Briefly discuss the life of St Francis of Assisi or another saint, before they begin work.
>
> **Extension:** Let pairs do their own research on the life of St Francis of Assisi or another Catholic saint in preparation.

2. A dramatic escape

> **Objective**
> To summarise the main ideas drawn from more than one paragraph.
>
> **What you need**
> Copies of *The Wolf Wilder*.
>
> **Cross-curricular link**
> Art and design

What to do

- Re-read Chapter 7 from 'The neighing did not begin again' as far as 'I think so. But not yet'.

- Tell the children to imagine they are preparing to film this section for a movie. Explain that filmmakers often make storyboards before filming: a sequence of pictures showing how the action develops. Write on the board the headings 'Characters', 'Setting' and 'Action'. Explain that each scene in a storyboard summarises what is happening.

- Arrange the children into pairs and tell them to skim and scan this section and decide on six scenes which they are going to illustrate for their storyboard. They should write notes on what each scene should depict using the headings on the board. Encourage them to include detail such as sound effects (the horse screaming, the clattering icicles, Rakov's cries) and ideas for close-up camera shots.

- Bring the class back together and write the best suggestions on the board. Encourage feedback: where could a close-up shot be effective? (Rakov's face as the icicles descend; the four faces looking down at Feo when she re-joins them)

- Let the children, in their pairs, sketch the storyboard scenes they have briefed.

> **Differentiation**
> **Support:** Provide examples of things Feo and Ilya see, such as the winding road, the icicles, burned houses.
>
> **Extension:** Let the children choose another dramatic episode to storyboard.

3. Go figurative!

Objectives

To discuss and evaluate how authors use language, including figurative language, considering the impact on the reader; to select appropriate vocabulary, understanding how such choices can enhance meaning.

What you need

Copies of *The Wolf Wilder*, Extract 2, photocopiable page 42 'Go figurative!'

What to do

- Tell the children that they are going to focus on the author's language and, in particular, her use of figurative language, including similes and metaphors. Display Extract 2 and ask them to find an example of each ('The sky was the blue of winter palaces' – metaphor; 'the half-grown trees dipped like praying polar bears' – simile).

- Encourage the children to consider how the comparisons help the reader imagine the scene, and how much more effective the simile and metaphor are than saying simply 'the sky was a bright blue' and 'the trees were bowed down with snow'. Point out that in each case, the author has chosen to evoke other features of snowy landscapes: the bright blue colour of the paint used on the facades of Russian winter palaces, and white polar bears that live in the Arctic.

- Hand out photocopiable page 42 'Go figurative!' and let children work in pairs to complete it. When they have finished, bring the class back together to review their work. Ask: *Which phrases do you find most effective and why?*

- Challenge pairs to write a sentence using a simile or a metaphor to describe three things Feo and Ilya see on their journey.

Differentiation

Support: Limit the work to the photocopiable sheet.

Extension: Challenge pairs to write sentences using similes or metaphors describing characters or places in the novel.

4. Inventive Feo

Objectives

To select appropriate grammar and vocabulary; to use further organisational and presentational devices to guide the reader.

What you need

Copies of *The Wolf Wilder*, photocopiable page 43 'Inventive Feo'.

Cross-curricular link

Design and technology

What to do

- Arrange the class into pairs and challenge them to skim and scan the novel to find all the things that Feo makes or improvises during the course of the story (a compass, snow weapons, rich clothes, a bow and arrow, skis, waterproof shoes, wolf prints).

- Bring the class back together and list their ideas on the board. Explain that each pair should choose one of the articles and scan the text to extract simple instructions for making it. Try to ensure a broad range of choices across the class.

- Before they begin, revise some of the key features of writing instructions: choosing imperative or second-person verbs; setting out steps by using numbers, letters, or bullet points. Hand out photocopiable page 43 'Inventive Feo' and let them complete it in pairs.

- When they have finished, let pairs who have chosen the same article share their instructions, encouraging them to compare and contrast their work, collating ideas to get the most concise and effective instructions.

- If there is time, pairs can add diagrams or sketches to help the reader.

Differentiation

Support: Model one set of instructions, working together as a class before pairs begin.

Extension: Let pairs invent another item that Feo might make for the home or to use as a weapon against Rakov, and write instructions for making it.

5. Feo's diary

Objective
To select the appropriate form for the purpose of the writing.

What you need
Copies of *The Wolf Wilder*.

Cross-curricular link
PSHE

What to do

- Explain to the children that they are going to recount events that happen to Feo in the form of a diary she might keep. Briefly review key features of diary writing (use of first-person verbs; past tense; informal writing; may include reflective/subjective emotions). Ask: *Can you think of any famous books that are written in diary form?* (*The Diary of a Young Girl* by Anne Frank, *The Diary of a Killer Cat* by Anne Fine and *Diary of a Wimpy Kid* by Jeff Kinney, for example.)

- Let them work in pairs to choose a significant day in the novel to recount (perhaps, the day General Rakov visits; the day of the party when Ilya dances, and so on).

- Let them then work individually to scan the text for what Feo might include in her diary and what she might write about her emotions and feelings. (For example, she might record how amazed and proud she felt when she watched Ilya dance.)

- When they have drafted their diary entries, let them compare and contrast them with their writing partner's entry, deciding what is effective and how they could be improved.

- Invite volunteers to read their diary entries, and encourage constructive feedback.

Differentiation

Support: Provide question prompts that children can refer to when they are writing their diary entries. For example, ask: *What are the main events that happen? How do they make Feo feel?*

Extension: The children can write another entry describing a different significant day or write about the same day from another character's perspective.

6. A wolf's story

Objectives
To predict what might happen from details stated and implied; to use other similar writing as models for their own.

What you need
Copies of *The Wolf Wilder*.

What to do

- Discuss how when a novel becomes popular, an author may write another book – or sequel – featuring the same character/s but developing a new narrative. Encourage the children to cite novels, or films, that have sequels. Tell them that sometimes the author chooses to develop a plot following one of the other characters featured in the first novel.

- Tell them that they are going to develop ideas for a sequel to *The Wolf Wilder*, about another wolf that Feo wilds. Brainstorm some ideas for the plot together as a class.

- Ask children to make notes for their sequel. Suggest that the novel could begin with the character recounting its past life as a pet. Encourage them to refer to the preface note on wolf wilders for ideas. Encourage them to explore different pathways for the narrative (for example, the wolf might become lost or get into danger).

- When they have finished, ask them to write the opening paragraph of their story. Before they begin, they should re-read the first pages of the novel, as far as 'It all began… with someone knocking on the snow-blue door'. Encourage them to adopt the same 'fairy-tale' style of the novel for their sequel.

Differentiation

Support: Develop ideas for one pathway as a class activity. Then let children write the opening paragraph together.

Extension: Challenge children to draft another paragraph or a chapter from their sequel.

A new saint

- Use this page to develop the idea for a saint of wolf pups.

Name _____

Where and when he or she lived

_____

_____

_____

What good deeds did they do?

_____

_____

_____

_____

Who or what might people believe they protect?

_____

_____

Write a few lines of a prayer that Feo offers to the saint.

_____

_____

_____

_____

_____

_____

Go figurative!

- Choose the correct word to match each description and write it in the correct space.
- Then write a sentence in the box to explain the comparison.

running	snow	dancing	food

Word and description	Explain the comparison
the most talkative weather there is	
writing with your feet	
the only thing more important than justice	
walking, only more of it	

Now think of three or more other things Feo and Ilya saw on their journey. On a separate piece of paper, write your own similes or metaphors to describe them.

Inventive Feo

- Write Feo's instructions for something useful she makes in the novel.

What is it? _____

Why is it needed? _____

_____

What you need to make it:

_____

_____

_____

_____

_____

How to make it (add more numbered steps, or don't use them all, if necessary)

1. _____

_____

2. _____

_____

3. _____

_____

4. _____

_____

5. _____

_____

- Use another sheet to sketch the design. Remember to add labels.

ASSESSMENT ▶

1. Top themes

> ### Objectives
> To identify and discuss themes; to make comparisons across books.
>
> ### What you need
> Copies of *The Wolf Wilder*.
>
> ### Cross-curricular link
> PSHE

What to do

- Ask the children what they think are the main themes in the novel (friendship with animals; the beginnings of the Russian Revolution; the bravery and strength of children). Write ideas on the board, prompting with questions such as: *What does the author suggest about children? What does she suggest was going on in Russia a hundred years ago?*

- Invite comparisons with other novels the class has read that cover similar themes (for example, friendship or animal friends), focusing on key features such as plot and style, and encouraging subjective opinion ('I think this is more exciting/ unusual/interesting because…').

- Ask children to choose the theme they think is most significant. They should draft a short statement beginning 'I think *The Wolf Wilder* is a novel about…', describing the theme and why they think it is important. (For example, 'I think *The Wolf Wilder* is about being brave and standing up for what you believe in, as Feo stands up to the cruel General and rescues her mother.')

- Invite volunteers to read out their statements, and encourage feedback.

> ### Differentiation
> **Support:** Provide a list of key themes on the board then ask them to choose the one they think is most significant and draft a statement.
>
> **Extension:** Children can construct mind maps showing main themes in the novel, with notes about each.

2. Plot picks

> ### Objective
> To summarise the main ideas drawn from more than one paragraph.
>
> ### What you need
> Copies of *The Wolf Wilder*; flash cards with names of key characters: Feo, Ilya, Alexei, Marina, Rakov; stopwatch; photocopiable page 47 'Plot picks'.

What to do

- Tell the children they are going to try to summarise how key characters are important to the plot in as concise a way as possible. Explain that you will hold up flash cards with characters' names, and volunteers should then summarise in as few words as possible, and in under 30 seconds, how they are important to the plot. They should follow this sentence pattern: 'Ilya is important to the plot because…'.

- Model one example for them: *Ilya is important to the plot because he ignores his orders to kill wolves and warns Feo and Marina that Rakov is coming, then helps Feo escape and rescue her mother from jail.*

- Challenge each volunteer to summarise key points in under 30 seconds, using the stopwatch.

- Tell the children they are now going to do the same exercise, focusing on objects that are important in the plot. Hand out photocopiable page 47 'Plot picks' and allow children time to complete it.

> ### Differentiation
> **Support:** Before children begin the written work, allow them to discuss the context of each item on the sheet in pairs.
>
> **Extension:** Challenge children to extend the sheet by sketching other items that feature in the plot, briefly explaining their significance.

3. Chapter and content

Objectives
To précis longer passages; to summarise the main ideas drawn from more than one paragraph.

What you need
Copies of *The Wolf Wilder*.

What to do

- Review the way the novel is organised, reminding the children of the section breaks marked by paw prints. Point out that the author has only used chapter numbers, not titles. Tell the children they are going to skim and scan the chapters and think up titles for them. Reflect on what a chapter title needs to do before they begin (give readers an idea of the content of the chapter without giving away too much of the plot, and act as a hook to make them want to read on).

- Together, discuss some ideas for chapter titles and write them on the board: for example, Chapter 4 might be 'An unwelcome visitor' or 'A threat'.

- Arrange the children into small groups and assign each group three or four chapters. They should skim and scan each chapter to remind themselves of what happens and come up with a suitable title. Allow them time to think up and list their ideas then bring the class back together to review their suggestions.

- Encourage constructive feedback and criticism. Ask: *Which titles are most effective and why?*

Differentiation
Support: Choose four chapters from the novel and skim and scan them as a shared activity to create ideas for titles.

Extension: Challenge children to group chapters into different parts or sections of the novel and think up titles for the parts.

4. A Russian glossary

Objectives
To understand the spelling of some words needs to be learned specifically; to explore the meaning of words in context.

What you need
Copies of *The Wolf Wilder*, dictionaries.

Cross-curricular links
Geography, history

What to do

- Tell the children they are going to compile a glossary of words which will help readers understand the author's references to the setting and time period of the novel (Russia, in the years running up to the revolution).

- Assign small groups four or five chapters each and tell them to skim and scan the chapters for any words which specifically relate to the time or place, and which readers today might not instantly recognise or understand. (For example, 'The Tsar'; 'Lenin'; 'dachas', an 'agitator', 'serfs', and so on. They can also include Russian words such as *'lapushka'* – darling.) They should list all the words they can find and then together create a definition for each word which would explain it clearly and concisely to readers who are unfamiliar with the word or context.

- When the groups have finished, allow them time to check their definitions using dictionaries. They should then use their word list to test other groups on tricky spellings and meanings.

- Finally, let groups share their findings to compile a glossary for the novel.

- Review the glossary as a class, encouraging children to edit and improve their work.

Differentiation
Support: Allow children to use dictionaries to help them find definitions.

Extension: Challenge groups to use their own reading and research to extend their glossaries.

5. Time for a test

Objective
To ask relevant questions to extend their understanding and knowledge.

What you need
Copies of *The Wolf Wilder*.

What to do

- Tell the children they are going to compile multiple-choice quiz questions about the novel to challenge other groups or teams. Arrange them into small groups and allow time to compile a quiz of six multiple-choice questions. Children should skim and scan the novel for ideas for questions. They should appoint one note-taker to write down their questions and another to keep a list of correct answers.

- Before they begin, model an example on the board:

  Feo makes a grave for:
  a)   Tenderfoot
  b)   Grey
  c)   The dead wolf pup   Answer: b)

- Groups can then challenge each other to answer their quiz questions. Again, they will need to appoint a note-taker to count correct or incorrect answers.

- When they have finished, review scores and announce winning teams or groups. Encourage feedback, identifying which quiz questions were most challenging and why (for example, where the names of characters or wolves could be confused).

- Allow groups time to compete in a Spelling Bee challenge: each should compile six of the trickiest spellings they can find in the novel, and challenge other groups to spell them from memory.

Differentiation
Support: Provide some possible questions for the quiz and ask children to come up with three answer options (only one of which is correct).

Extension: Ask groups of children to devise an alternative quiz (such as a true-or-false quiz) about the novel to challenge other groups.

6. Book club

Objectives
To explain and discuss their understanding of what they have read; to articulate and justify opinions.

What you need
Copies of *The Wolf Wilder*.

What to do

- Explain that the children are going to pretend they are taking part in a book-club programme on the radio to review the novel.

- Discuss some questions that the programme's presenter might ask, and list them on the board. For example: *Did you enjoy the novel and if so, why? What is your favourite part of the novel and why? Do you like the main character, Feo? Would this novel encourage you to read others by the same author and, if so, why?*

- Allow them time to work on their own to prepare some notes on what they think or feel about the novel. Encourage them to refer to the novel and to back up their views with evidence, for example: 'I like Feo because she shows girls can be strong and fearless and it is not only boys who can be heroes.'

- Appoint a presenter or presenters who will give a brief introduction to the book, and then invite others to participate in a group discussion about the novel. The presenter can use the questions on the board and add more of their own.

Differentiation
Support: Children could discuss their opinions of the novel in pairs before they begin the book-club discussion.

Extension: Children could follow up the discussion by drafting a review for a newspaper or website.

Plot picks

- Briefly explain how each of the following feature in the plot.

_____
_____
_____
_____

_____
_____
_____
_____

_____
_____
_____
_____
_____

_____
_____
_____
_____
_____

_____
_____
_____
_____

_____
_____
_____
_____

- Choose one item which you think is most important to the plot and explain why.

_____
_____
_____
_____
_____
_____

SCHOLASTIC
READ & RESPOND

Available in this series:

Key Stage 1

978-1407-18254-4

978-1407-16053-5

978-1407-14220-3

978-1407-15875-4

978-1407-16058-0

Key Stage 2

978-1407-14228-9

978-1407-14224-1

978-1407-14229-6

978-14071-6057-3

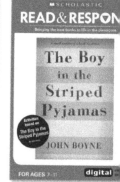

978-14071-6071-9

978-14071-6069-6

978-14071-6067-2

978-14071-4231-9

978-14071-4223-4

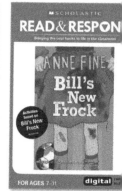

978-14071-6060-3

978-14071-5876-1

978-14071-6068-9

978-14071-6063-4

978-1407-18253-7

978-1407-18252-0

To find out more, call 0845 6039091
or visit our website www.scholastic.co.uk/readandrespond